**W9-AOK-767**

# STEWARDSHIP OF TALENT

S T A N   T O L E R

Special thanks to: Mark Graham, Steve Weber,
Terry Toler, Derl Keefer, Jeffrey Johnson,
and Deloris Leonard

# FOREWORD

How many times have you wondered what could be accomplished for the kingdom of God if His people were completely dedicated to using their God-given talents for His purposes? This little book, authored by my good friend Stan Toler, is filled with morsels of wisdom to incite us to hone our talents so that God might better use them. Read it, draw from its insights, and share them with others. You and those around you will be the better for it.

This book is the third in a series of a stewardship trilogy by Stan Toler. If you have not yet been exposed to the first two books of this trilogy, you will want to read *Stewardship Starters*\* (on the subject of finance) and *Stewardship of Time*.\*\* Ultimately, we must all come to terms with the basic stewardship challenge that our time, talent, and treasure are on loan from God. May each of us learn to better manage these resources provided by our loving Lord. Thanks to Dr. Toler for compiling these simple, yet profound, words of stewardship wisdom.

Steve Weber
Director
Stewardship Development Ministries
Church of the Nazarene

# INTRODUCTION

The concept of skill might be as old as the earth, but the actual English word is a mere sapling. The word *skill* originated with Old Norse language in Scandinavia from the root words *skil, skal, skilha,* and *schill.* Generally these words referred to using reason or intellect to make a difference. As time passed, they came to speak of the ability to use one's knowledge effectively and readily in the performance of some task.

Today, skill relates more to the use of physical abilities or talent. God called Adam and Eve to use their abilities in the garden to "work it and take care of it" (Gen. 2:15). He continues to call us to use those gifts and graces He has provided us to benefit His kingdom, others, and ourselves.

What do the Scriptures say about talent? What do we do with it? The following quotes are aimed at helping us to grasp the value of our talents and to encourage us to find creative ways to sharpen and use them for God. My prayer is that when we stand before Him at the Judgment, He will consider us to have been good stewards of the skills He gave us.

You are loved!

Stan Toler
Eph. 3:20-21

For by the grace given me I say to every one of you: Do not think of yourself more highly than you ought, but rather think of yourself with sober judgment, in accordance with the measure of faith God has given you. Just as each of us has one body with many members, and these members do not all have the same function, so in Christ we who are many form one body, and each member belongs to all the others. We have different gifts, according to the grace given us. If a man's gift is prophesying, let him use it in proportion to his faith. If it is serving, let him serve; if it is teaching, let him teach; if it is encouraging, let him encourage; if it is contributing to the needs of others, let him give generously; if it is leadership, let him govern diligently; if it is showing mercy, let him do it cheerfully.

*Rom. 12:3-8*

❦ The price of greatness is responsibility.

❦ But he that is greatest among you shall be your servant.

*Matt. 23:11*

❦ There is that which we hold in our hands, of possessions and influence, which are to be no longer held as unto ourselves or so as to revolve around ourselves; they are to be melted into our life's devotement unto Jesus Christ.

*P. F. Bresee*

❦ Therefore, as we have opportunity, let us do good to all people, especially to those who belong to the family of believers.

*Gal. 6:10*

❦ What I kept, I lost,
What I spent, I had,
What I gave, I have.

*Persian proverb*

It is possible to give without loving, but it is impossible to love without giving.

*Richard Braunstein*

For this reason I remind you to fan into flame the gift of God, which is in you through the laying on of my hands.

*2 Tim. 1:6*

No man is born into the world whose work is not born with him; there is always work, and tools to work . . . for those who will.

*James Russell Lowell*

Greatness lies not in being strong, but in the right use of strength.

Christian giving is God's divine plan to make us like himself; it reveals our religion and bares our souls; it is prophetic and has to do with the inner sensitiveness and gives a keener vision to His work and plans.

*Warren H. Denison*

What you give to humanity you get back. Bread cast upon the waters is much more wholesome and nourishing than pie in the sky.

*Melvin Jones*

❧ Keep me safe, O God, for in you I take refuge.

*Ps. 16:1*

❧ Talents are best nurtured in solitude; but character is best formed in the strong billows of the world.

*Johann Wolfgang von Goethe*

O Lord, there is plenty of money, seemingly, for the great churches out in this part of the city. I would that Thou wouldst give me some money to make a place for the Church of the Nazarene. Immediately, as though a voice from heaven, there were uttered in my very consciousness the words, "I have given myself to you." I said, "Thank God, that is enough! I would rather have Thee than all else, and with Thee we have all things."

*P. F. Bresee*
*Founder, Church of the Nazarene*

To know the will of God is the greatest knowledge, to find the will of God is the greatest discovery, and to do the will of God is the greatest achievement.

*W. A. Criswell*

This is how we know what love is: Jesus Christ laid down his life for us. And we ought to lay down our lives for our brothers.

*1 John 3:16*

God's gifts put man's best dreams to shame.

*Elizabeth Barrett Browning*

We judge ourselves by what we feel capable of doing, while others judge us by what we have already done.

*Henry Wadsworth Longfellow*

But the seed on good soil stands for those with a noble and good heart, who hear the word, retain it, and by persevering produce a crop.

*Luke 8:15*

God has given us two hands—one to receive with and the other to give with. We are not cisterns made for hoarding; we are channels made for sharing.

*Billy Graham*

❦ Are you relying on yourself or on God to help you in the key areas of your life? It's a question to ask yourself today—and every day.

❦ The world asks, How much does he give? Christ asks, Why does he give?

*John R. Mott*

❦ For God did not give us a spirit of timidity, but a spirit of power, of love and of self-discipline.

*2 Tim. 1:7*

## ✿ *Servanthood*

Everybody can be great. Because anybody can serve. You don't have to have a college degree to serve. You don't have to make your subject and your verb agree to serve. . . . You only need a heart full of grace. A soul generated by love.

*Martin Luther King Jr.*

### ❦ *Scripture*

Most people are bothered by those Scripture passages that they cannot understand. But for me, the passages in Scripture that trouble me most are those that I do understand.

*Mark Twain*

Thank God every morning when you get up that you have something to do that day which must be done whether you like it or not. Being forced to work and forced to do your best will breed in you a hundred virtues which the idle will never know.

*Charles Kingsley*

❦ Many people quench the Spirit by being down in the mouth rather than rejoicing, by planning rather than praying, by murmuring rather than giving thanks, and by worrying instead of trusting in Him who is faithful.

*Cameron Townsend*
*Founder, Wycliffe Bible Translators*

We must not dictate to Jesus as to where we are going to serve Him. There is a theory abroad today that we have to consecrate our gifts to God. We cannot, they are not ours to consecrate; every gift we have has been given to us. Jesus Christ does not take my gifts and use them; He takes me and turns me right about-face, and realizes himself in me for His glory.

*Oswald Chambers*

Freely you have received, freely give.
*Matt. 10:8*

❦ The man who is born with a talent that he was meant to use finds his greatest happiness in using it.

❦ Do not merely listen to the word, and so deceive yourselves. Do what it says.

*James 1:22*

Ah, to be your instrument, O God,
like Paul to the Gentiles,
like Philip to the eunuch,
like Jesus to the world,
. . . to be your instrument.
To be like a scalpel in the gentle hands of a surgeon,
healing and mending.
To be like a plow in the weathered hands of a
  farmer,
sowing and tending.
To be like a scythe in the sweeping hands of a
  reaper,
gathering and using.

To be . . . an instrument for noble purposes.
To be honed and tuned,
in sync with your will,
sensitive to your touch.
This, my God, is my prayer.
Draw me from your fire,
form me on your anvil,
shape me with your hands,
and let me be your tool.

*Max Lucado,*
On the Anvil, *p. 107*

❀ A man's pride brings him low, but a man of lowly spirit gains honor.

*Prov. 29:23*

❀ Deeds, not stones, are the true monuments of the great.

❦ Now Daniel so distinguished himself among the administrators and the satraps by his exceptional qualities that the king planned to set him over the whole kingdom.

*Dan. 6:3*

Now it is required that those who have been given a trust must prove faithful.

*1 Cor. 4:2*

Honor the LORD with your wealth, with the firstfruits of all your crops; then your barns will be filled to overflowing, and your vats will brim over with new wine.

*Prov. 3:9-10*

Whether you think you can or whether you think you can't, you're right.

*Henry Ford*

33

When our capabilities are of God, we are never incapable.

*Chuck Millhuff*

Whoever serves me must follow me; and where I am, my servant also will be. My Father will honor the one who serves me.

*John 12:26*

However, I consider my life worth nothing to me, if only I may finish the race and complete the task the Lord Jesus has given me—the task of testifying to the gospel of God's grace.

*Acts 20:24*

God considers two factors in recruiting servants: (1) the particular ministry needs; and (2) the person who perfectly fits the servant profile. God chose Abraham because he was the only man alive who would outwait unbelief to gain his patrimony. He chose Noah because only he could see thunderstorms in skies that had never floated a cloud. He chose David because although king-designate, he was willing to serve as public enemy number one. He chose Hannah because she freely surrendered her only hope of happiness just as she had promised she would. He chose Ezekiel because no one else would act like a lunatic in order to bring Israel to her senses. He chose Mary because she alone believed that God could outwit the law of human regeneration.

God has numerous ministries that need to be serviced. Which one of us would be willing to offer our résumé to check against the servant profile?

*Virgl Hurley*
Dallas Speakers Sourcebook
*Word, 1995*

As the purse is emptied, the heart is filled.
*Victor Hugo*

Whoever believes in me, as the Scripture has said, streams of living water will flow from within him.

*John 7:38*

## *Definition of Talent*

The abilities, powers, and gifts bestowed upon a man : natural endowments <the stewardship of your time, *talent*, and treasure> <the *talents* which God has given you as a divine trust>

Webster's Third New International Dictionary

## ❦ *A Leader's Prayer*

Dear God, with Your help I am able to see the hidden talents and abilities in those I work with. Please help me continually take action to encourage spiritual growth in their lives.

Time is my most valuable commodity. I take full responsibility to make sure I maximize my use of it to enhance my life and further my vision.

*Zig Ziglar*

❦ Then he said to them, "Watch out! Be on your guard against all kinds of greed; a man's life does not consist in the abundance of his possessions."

*Luke 12:15*

❦ Talent that is used is multiplied.

*Steve Weber*

Do all the good you can,
By all the means you can,
In all the ways you can,
In all the places you can,
At all the times you can,
To all the people you can,
As long as ever you can.

*John Wesley*

❀ The good man brings good things out of the good stored up in him, and the evil man brings evil things out of the evil stored up in him.

*Matt. 12:35*

❀ Talent is the capacity of doing anything that depends on application and industry; it is voluntary power, while genius is involuntary.

*Hazlett*

Jesus replied, "Love the Lord your God with all your heart and with all your soul and with all your mind."

*Matt. 22:37*

Ability involves responsibility. Power to its last particle is duty.

*Alexander Maclaren*

❦ The plans of the diligent lead to profit as surely as haste leads to poverty.

*Prov. 21:5*

❦ What I gave, I have. What I saved and what I spent, I lost.

*Graveyard epitaph*

❦ Finally, be strong in the Lord and in his mighty power.

*Eph. 6:10*

❦ It is possible to be too big for God to use you, but never too small for God to use you.

*Melvin Maxwell*

❀ Then Caleb silenced the people before Moses and said, "We should go up and take possession of the land, for we can certainly do it." But the men who had gone up with him said, "We can't attack those people; they are stronger than we are."

*Num. 13:30-31*

❀ The true value of money is not in its possession, but in its use.

*Aesop*

But by the grace of God I am what I am, and his grace to me was not without effect. No, I worked harder than all of them—yet not I, but the grace of God that was with me.

*1 Cor. 15:10*

❧ Beware of the tendency of trying to do what God alone can do, and of blaming God for not doing what we alone can do.

*Oswald Chambers*

❧ Jesus Christ calls service what we are to Him, not what we do for Him.

*Oswald Chambers*

If you want to be of use to God, get rightly related to Jesus Christ.

*R. S. Nicholson*

Looking for opportunities to serve God is an imperative every time, and all the time is our opportunity of serving God.

*Oswald Chambers*

Any work for God that has less than a passion for Jesus Christ as its motive will end in crushing heartache and discouragement.

*John R. Church*

The greatest service we can render to God is to fulfill our spiritual destiny.

*Loren Gresham*

❦ The gifted whose work speaks for God is the one who realizes what God has done in him.

*Mendell Taylor*

❦ The value of our work depends on whether we can direct people to Jesus Christ.

*Nate Krupp*

Christian service is not our work; loyalty to Jesus is our work.

*David Lattimer*

I have no business in God's service if I have any personal reserve; I must be broken bread and poured-out wine in His hands.

*Oswald Chambers*

54

We need leaders who empower people and create other leaders. It is no longer good enough for a leader to make sure that everybody has something to do and is producing.

*Farzin Madjidi*

In a large house there are articles not only of gold and silver, but also of wood and clay; some are for noble purposes and some for ignoble. If a man cleanses himself from the latter, he will be an instrument for noble purposes, made holy, useful to the Master and prepared to do any good work.

*2 Tim. 2:20-21*

❦ You can't hold a man down staying down with him.

*Vance Havner*

❦ God, please give me something that I can give to others.

*A gifted leader's prayer*

❦ We are created and called to minister.

*Jim Garlow*

❦ Therefore, if anyone is in Christ, he is a new creation; the old has gone, the new has come! All this is from God, who reconciled us to himself through Christ and gave us the ministry of reconciliation: that God was reconciling the world to himself in Christ, not counting men's sins against them. And he has committed to us the message of reconciliation. We are therefore Christ's ambassadors, as though God were making his appeal through us. We implore you on Christ's behalf: Be reconciled to God. God made him who had no sin to be sin for us, so that in him we might become the righteousness of God.

*2 Cor. 5:17-21*

❦ Every member should be a minister.
*Rick Warren*

❦ Do not neglect your gift, which was given you through a prophetic message when the body of elders laid their hands on you.
*1 Tim. 4:14*

❀ Nobody makes a greater mistake than he who did nothing because he could only do a little.

*Edmund Burke*

❀ The only investments I ever made that have paid constantly increasing dividends are those I have given to the Lord's work.

*J. L. Kraft*

It was he who gave some to be apostles, some to be prophets, some to be evangelists, and some to be pastors and teachers, to prepare God's people for works of service, so that the body of Christ may be built up.

*Eph. 4:11-12*

The Gift of God is the Son of God; the gift from the Gift of God is the Holy Spirit.

*Oswald Chambers*

We have nothing to do with what gifts we possess, or how many. But we have everything to do with how we use them.

*John C. Maxwell*

Now he who supplies seed to the sower and bread for food will also supply and increase your store of seed and will enlarge the harvest of your righteousness. You will be made rich in every way so that you can be generous on every occasion, and through us your generosity will result in thanksgiving to God.

*2 Cor. 9:10-11*

So we say with confidence:
"The Lord is my helper; I will not be afraid.
What can man do to me?"

*Heb. 13:6*

Our greatest ambition in life should be to please God.

*Paul White*

❦ Therefore the LORD, the God of Israel, declares: "I promised that your house and your father's house would minister before me forever." But now the LORD declares: "Far be it from me! Those who honor me I will honor, but those who despise me will be disdained."

*1 Sam. 2:30*

❦ This service that you perform is not only supplying the needs of God's people but is also overflowing in many expressions of thanks to God.

*2 Cor. 9:12*

❦ So if you have not been trustworthy in handling worldly wealth, who will trust you with true riches?

*Luke 16:11*

We have the notion that we can consecrate our gifts to God. You cannot consecrate what is not yours; there is only one thing you can consecrate to God, and that is your right to yourself. If you will give God your right to yourself, He will make a holy experiment out of you. God's experiments always succeed.

*Oswald Chambers*

❦ There are no victories at bargain prices.
*Dwight Eisenhower*

❦ To bring one's self to a frame of mind and to the proper energy to accomplish things that require plain hard work continuously is the one big battle that everyone has. When this battle is won for all time, then everything is easy.

*Thomas A. Buckner*

Too many Christians say, "God will provide." The good news is, "He already has provided, He gives to His people." The bad news is, "His people many times do not want to let go of it."

*Orville Hagan*

❦ Use what talent you possess: The woods would be very silent if no birds sang there except those that sang best.

*Henry van Dyke*

❦ It is almost as presumptuous to think you can do nothing as to think you can do everything.

*Dave Sutherland*

Consider the postage stamp: Its usefulness consists in the ability to stick to one thing till it gets there.

*Josh Bellize*

After they had heard the king, they went on their way, and the star they had seen in the east went ahead of them until it stopped over the place where the child was. When they saw the star, they were overjoyed. On coming to the house, they saw the child with his mother Mary, and they bowed down and worshiped him. Then they opened their treasures and presented him with gifts of gold and of incense and of myrrh. And having been warned in a dream not to go back to Herod, they returned to their country by another route.

*Matt. 2:9-12*

❦ Gold is a gift for a king.
Frankincense is a gift for a spirit.
Myrrh is a gift for one who is dying.

❦ Jesus came into the world to live for men, and, in the end, to die for men. He came to give for men His life and His death.

*James Diehl*

Talent is cheap; dedication is costly!
*Michelangelo*

We have nothing to do with how much ability we've got, or how little, but with what we do with what we have.

*Gary Inrig*

For everyone who has will be given more, and he will have an abundance. Whoever does not have, even what he has will be taken from him. And throw that worthless servant outside, into the darkness, where there will be weeping and gnashing of teeth.

*Matt. 25:29-30*

❀ One's stewardship is a privileged responsibility for which he will be held accountable.
*Brian Kluth*

❀ Both the opportunity to do ministry and be rewarded is a testimony to the grace of God.
*Derl Keefer*

There is a danger of hoarding that which God wants me to invest for eternal priorities.

*Amos Henry*

During the absence of Christ, believers should work diligently with the abilities entrusted to them.

*Doug Carter*

The realities of future judgment ought to promote faithful efforts in the present.

*P. O. Carpenter*

The man who goes alone can start the day. But he who travels with another must wait until the other is ready.

*Henry David Thoreau*

Flatter me, and I may not believe you. Criticize me, and I may not like you. Ignore me, and I may not forgive you. Encourage me, and I will not forget you.

*William Arthur Ward*

After the person has become successful, you switch from giving permission to making it a responsibility. You say, "God's given you something to develop. It's your responsibility to take that and do as much as you can with it."

*Fred Smith*

❀ God has made us from the dust, but He doesn't intend for us to live there.

*Fred Smith*

❀ People have a "need to succeed" in them. Most never find it.

*John C. Maxwell*

❦ The world wants your best, but God wants your all.

*W. Talmadge Johnson*

❦ Let us not become weary in doing good, for at the proper time we will reap a harvest if we do not give up.

*Gal. 6:9*

❧ Talent is that which is in a man's power; genius is that in whose power a man is.

*Lowell Lundstrom*

❧ Woe to the man who receives a talent and ties it in a napkin.

*Jerome*

❦ Every good and perfect gift is from above, coming down from the Father of the heavenly lights, who does not change like shifting shadows.

*James 1:17*

❦ No one knows what he can do till he tries.
*Publilius Syrus*

❦ Brothers, I do not consider myself yet to have taken hold of it. But one thing I do: Forgetting what is behind and straining toward what is ahead.

*Phil. 3:13*

❦ Study, practice, and work so that your life will be as effective as possible.

*Steve Green*

If a man has a talent and cannot use it, he has failed. If he has a talent and uses only half of it, he has partly failed. If he has a talent and learns somehow to use the whole of it, he has gloriously succeeded and has a satisfaction and a triumph few men ever know.

*Thomas Wolfe*

Give strength, give thought, give deeds,
   give wealth;
Give love, give tears, and give thyself.
Give, give, be always giving.
Who gives not is not living;
The more you give, the more you live.

*Anonymous*

Because judgment without mercy will be shown to anyone who has not been merciful. Mercy triumphs over judgment!

*James 2:13*

There are three kinds of giving: grudge giving, duty giving, and thanksgiving. Grudge giving says, "I hate to," duty giving says, "I ought to," thanksgiving says, "I want to." The first comes from constraint, the second comes from a sense of obligation, the third from a full heart. Nothing much is conveyed in grudge giving, since "the gift without the giver is bare." Something more happens in duty giving, but there is no song in it. Thanksgiving is an open gate into the love of God.

*Robert N. Rodenmayer,*
Thanks Be to God

God always begins with us where we are.
*John Conley*

We can expect the works of God to become magnified through that which has been given to God.

*Keith Wright*

By their fruit you will recognize them. Do people pick grapes from thornbushes, or figs from thistles?

*Matt. 7:16*

One of the great gifts a leader can give to others is to lift them up. The problem with too many people in leadership positions is that they want to lift themselves up above people.

*LeBron Fairbanks*

Therefore everyone who hears these words of mine and puts them into practice is like a wise man who built his house on the rock. The rain came down, the streams rose, and the winds blew and beat against that house; yet it did not fall, because it had its foundation on the rock. But everyone who hears these words of mine and does not put them into practice is like a foolish man who built his house on sand. The rain came down, the streams rose, and the wind blew and beat against that house, and it fell with a great crash.

*Matt. 7:24-27*

Early in the morning, as he was on his way back to the city, he was hungry. Seeing a fig tree by the road, he went up to it but found nothing on it except leaves. Then he said to it, "May you never bear fruit again!" Immediately the tree withered. When the disciples saw this, they were amazed. "How did the fig tree wither so quickly?" they asked. Jesus replied, "I tell you the truth, if you have faith and do not doubt, not only can you do what was done to the fig tree, but also you can say to this mountain, 'Go, throw yourself into the sea,' and it will be done. If you believe, you will receive whatever you ask for in prayer."

*Matt. 21:18-22*

The message of the fig tree is not for all of us to have the same fruit. The message is for us to have some fruit. Not easy!

*Max Lucado*

You can't take people where you haven't been.

*Larry Huch*

The truth is this: Spiritual maturity is demonstrated more by behavior than by beliefs. The Christian life isn't just a matter of creeds and convictions; it includes conduct and character. Beliefs must be backed up with behavior.

*Rick Warren*

Do not get drunk on wine, which leads to debauchery. Instead, be filled with the Spirit.

*Eph. 5:18*

Believers grow faster when you provide a track to grow on.

*Elmer Towns*

God never asks about our ability or our inability—just our availability.

*Charles Fletcher*

Then I heard the voice of the Lord saying, "Whom shall I send? And who will go for us?" And I said, "Here am I. Send me!"

*Isa. 6:8*

If we work upon marble, it will perish; if we work upon bronze, time will efface it; if we build temples, they will crumble into dust; but if we work upon immortal souls, if we imbue them with just principles of action, with fear of wrong and love of right, we engrave on those tables something which no time can obliterate, and which will brighten through all eternity. Give what truly will last—a witness of Christ.

*Daniel Webster*

In the same way, let your light shine before men, that they may see your good deeds and praise your Father in heaven.

*Matt. 5:16*

Too many people make cemeteries of their lives by burying their talents.

*G. B. Williamson*

Many people have ability but lack stability.
*David Case*

The real tragedy of life is not in being limited to one talent, but in the failure to use the one talent.

*Edgar W. Work*

The greatest gifts we can give to others are not material things but gifts of ourselves. The great gifts are those of love, of inspiration, of kindness, of encouragement, of forgiveness, of ideas and ideals.

*Walter A. Heiby*

❀ I do not believe in circumstances. The people who get on in this world are the people who get up and look for the circumstances they want, and, if they cannot find them, make them.

*George Bernard Shaw*

True, everything we have comes from our Father, our ability, our industry, our technical know-how. But when we use it without Him, when we treat it as paid-out capital that we can use as we please, it decays in our hands.

*Helmut Thielicke*

## 🎗 *A Round Tuit*

This is a Tuit. Guard it with your life, as Tuits are hard to come by, especially the round ones. This is an indispensable item. It will help you become a more efficient worker. For years we have heard people say, "I'll do it as soon as I get a Round Tuit." Now that you have one, you can accomplish all those things you put aside until you got a Round Tuit!

*Unknown*

Success is to be measured not so much by the position that one has reached in life as by the obstacles that one has overcome while trying to succeed.

*Booker T. Washington*

Words of encouragement fan the spark of genius into the flame of achievement. Legend tells us that Lincoln's dying mother called her small son to her bedside and whispered, "Be somebody, Abe!"

*Wilfred A. Peterson*

❦ Anything less than a conscious commitment to the important is an unconscious commitment to the unimportant.

*Stephen R. Covey*

❦ The true test of a first-rate mind is the ability to hold two contradictory ideas at the same time.

*F. Scott Fitzgerald*

The two hardest things to handle in life are failure and success.

*J. Michael Walters*

If you really want to do something, you'll find a way; if you don't, you'll find an excuse.

*Norman Vincent Peale*

❀ The happiest people don't necessarily have the best of everything. They just make the best of everything.

*Melvin Maxwell*

❀ Life is a place of service; joy can be real only if people look upon their life as a service and have a definite object in life outside themselves and their personal happiness.

*Leo Tolstoy*

## 🙰 *The Unyielded Life*

If you should visit the museum in Genoa, Italy, you would find in one room a glass case. Within this case there is an old violin, preserved under lock and key. It once was the property of Paganini, probably the world's greatest violinist. The instrument now renders no music. The time was, when in the hands of its owner, tones were produced that charmed and delighted vast audiences. Now this valuable old violin is silent. Even if its owner were alive today, he could produce no music from it, because it is locked up. In order to again produce those beautiful tones it must be unlocked, yielded into the hands of a violinist. May it not be that there are powers locked up within our souls and bodies that, if yielded to the Holy Ghost, would produce sweet music that would bless the world. Chords, no doubt, would vibrate that would cause us to rejoice with joy unspeakable and full of glory. But God cannot use our talents because they are locked up.

*James H. McConkey, in*
Holiness Illustrations
*by Leewin B. Williams*
*Kansas City: Beacon Hill Press, 1940*